This Discovery Journal Belongs to

_____

Begun: **Completed:**

Printed in the United States of America
First Printing, 2016

ISBN: 978-0-9890973-9-0

BISAC:
SEL027000 SELF-HELP / Personal Growth / Success
SEL045000 SELF-HELP / Journaling

Printed in the U.S.A.

Pyewacky Press
P.O. Box 265
Mendocino, CA 95460
katypye.com/pyewacky-press

Cover Illustration: © 2016 by Erin Summ
Cover design: Erin Summ and John Weston www.johncweston.com
Interior design & book production: Erin Summ and Pyewacky Press
Logo: John Weston www.johncweston.com
Cover and interior design images:
#103834744© PetarPaunchev – stock.adobe.com
#77938326 and #103834767 © Catwoman – stock.adobe.com
Author photo: Candace Smith www.candacesmithphotography.com

FOR YOU, THE SHY OR INTROVERTED
WOMAN ENTREPRENEUR

May you stand confident in who you are,
shine your brilliant light, and create the impact
you were born to make.

Shine
Glow
Change
dare
Courage
believe
proud
Value
empowered
impact
Love
self-love
Confident
light
Joy
powerful
valuable
soar
Bright
Life
thrive
mission
success
Self
Bold
Grow
Woman
Entrepreneur
Impact
Transform
breakthrough
pride
Vision
Proud
heart

INTRODUCTION

I am naturally shy, but growing up I knew I wanted my life to make a difference. After earning my Psychology degree, I launched my coaching career with a burning desire to serve women like me— shy or introverted women, especially struggling entrepreneurs on a mission. Women facing fears of being seen and heard. Women who know they are meant to be bigger than their barriers, meant to make an impact.

I took baby steps, then big leaps out of my comfort zone. It was scary, but over time and with practice, I gained the confidence to be bold and courageous. I did it for me and for you.

Journaling is a powerful tool for moving your dreams and desires out of your head, onto the page, and into your life.

WHAT COMPLETING THIS JOURNAL WILL HELP YOU DISCOVER

- that you have a life and message to share with the world
- that you are valuable and were born to make a special impact
- that you can learn to stand in confidence and courage, recognizing, accepting, and building on your natural gifts

THE WORK YOU WILL DO IN THIS JOURNAL

- discovering where you shine and where you hide your light
- uncovering barriers blocking your progress and success
- discovering ways to build confidence in yourself and your work
- building small, daily shifts into big change and steady growth

YOU CAN EXPECT TO

- gain confidence that who you are is all you need to shine
- diminish your fears so you feel safer being your true self
- realize new strategies or how to strengthen old ones to move toward your goals and vision on a solid foundation

11/12/16 #1 my intention is to keep pressing forward & holding myself accountable for my success.

Know what sparks the light in you. Then use that
light to illuminate the world. *Oprah Winfrey*

WHAT IS MY INTENTION FOR
THE NEXT 60 DAYS?

WHO AM I BEING NOW?

The roles we play in every area of our lives reflect how we see ourselves. Whether we let our true selves shine or hide is based on our background, specific situations, input from others, who we are with, and our day-to-day experiences.

What are the roles I play in my life? Spouse, parent, sibling, volunteer, entrepreneur, worker, friend, etc.? (*List the roles you play in the first column below. For each, check off whether your true self shines or hides.*)

ROLE	True Self Shines	True Self Hides

WHO AM I BEING NOW IN MY LIFE AND IN MY BUSINESS?

For the roles where you let your true self shine, what could you do to bring out even more of your true self?

WHO AM I BEING NOW
IN MY LIFE AND IN MY BUSINESS?

For the roles where your true self hides, what aspects of each hold you back from being your true self?

MY DAILY JOURNAL

AND

WEEKLY SUMMARIES

Date:

The quality of your life will be determined by
the questions you ask.   *Anthony Robbins*

Date:

Date:

What am I proud of myself for today?

Date:

Date:

What am I proud of myself for today?

Date:

Date:

What am I proud of myself for today?

Date:

Date:

What am I proud of myself for today?

Date:

Date:

What am I proud of myself for today?

Date:

Date:

What am I proud of myself for today?

Date:

WEEK #1
LOOK BACK

Where did I shine this week? What did I learn the most about myself, about my confidence this week?

When did I feel most vulnerable this week, and what did I do to feel more safe? Is this a strategy I can use again?

Why did I get in my way, shadow my light?

Who helped me break through a block, to stand strong, or see things in a new way? How?

What one thing will I do differently next week to boost my confidence and add steps toward my goals and dreams?

What am I grateful for this week?

Date:

Nothing blooms in your comfort zone. *Erin Summ*

Date:

Date:

What am I proud of myself for today?

Date:

Date:

What am I proud of myself for today?

Date:

Date:

What am I proud of myself for today?

Date:

Date:

What am I proud of myself for today?

Date:

Date:

What am I proud of myself for today?

Date:

Date:

What am I proud of myself for today?

Date:

WEEK #2
LOOK BACK

Where did I shine this week? What did I learn the most about myself, about my confidence this week?

When did I feel most vulnerable this week, and what did I do to feel more safe? Is this a strategy I can use again?

WEEK #2
LOOK BACK

Why did I get in my way, shadow my light?

Who helped me break through a block, to stand strong, or see things in a new way? How?

What one thing will I do differently next week to boost my confidence and add steps toward my goals and dreams?

What am I grateful for this week?

Date:

Most of the shadows in this life are caused by
standing in our own sunshine. *Ralph Waldo Emerson*

Date:

Date:

What am I proud of myself for today?

Date:

Date:

What am I proud of myself for today?

Date:

Date:

What am I proud of myself for today?

Date:

Date:

What am I proud of myself for today?

Date:

Date:

What am I proud of myself for today?

Date:

Date:

What am I proud of myself for today?

Date:

WEEK #3
LOOK BACK

Where did I shine this week? What did I learn the most about myself, about my confidence this week?

When did I feel most vulnerable this week, and what did I do to feel more safe? Is this a strategy I can use again?

WEEK #3
LOOK BACK

Why did I get in my way, shadow my light?

Who helped me break through a block, to stand strong, or see things in a new way? How?

What one thing will I do differently next week to boost my confidence and add steps toward my goals and dreams?

What am I grateful for this week?

Date:

It isn't where you come from, it's where you're
going that counts. *Ella Fitzgerald*

Date:

Date:

What am I proud of myself for today?

Date:

Date:

What am I proud of myself for today?

Date:

Date:

What am I proud of myself for today?

Date:

Date:

What am I proud of myself for today?

Date:

Date:

What am I proud of myself for today?

Date:

Date:

What am I proud of myself for today?

Date:

WEEK #4
LOOK BACK

Where did I shine this week? What did I learn the most about myself, about my confidence this week?

When did I feel most vulnerable this week, and what did I do to feel more safe? Is this a strategy I can use again?

WEEK #4
LOOK BACK

Why did I get in my way, shadow my light?

Who helped me break through a block, to stand strong, or see things in a new way? How?

What one thing will I do differently next week to boost my confidence and add steps toward my goals and dreams?

What am I grateful for this week?

Date:

As you think, so shall you become. *Bruce Lee*

Date:

Date:

What am I most grateful for today?

Date:

Date:

What am I proud of myself for today?

Date:

Date:

What am I proud of myself for today?

Date:

Date:

What am I proud of myself for today?

Date:

Date:

What am I proud of myself for today?

Date:

Date:

What am I proud of myself for today?

Date:

WEEK #5
LOOK BACK

Where did I shine this week? What did I learn the most about myself, about my confidence this week?

When did I feel most vulnerable this week, and what did I do to feel more safe? Is this a strategy I can use again?

WEEK #5
LOOK BACK

Why did I get in my way, shadow my light?

Who helped me break through a block, to stand strong, or see things in a new way? How?

What one thing will I do differently next week to boost my confidence and add steps toward my goals and dreams?

What am I grateful for this week?

 *Date:*

The sooner you learn to love who you are, the sooner you
will set free who you are meant to be. *Erin Summ*

Date:

Date:

What am I proud of myself for today?

Date:

Date:

What am I proud of myself for today?

Date:

Date:

What am I proud of myself for today?

Date:

Date:

What am I proud of myself for today?

Date:

Date:

What am I proud of myself for today?

Date:

Date:

What am I proud of myself for today?

Date:

WEEK #6
LOOK BACK

Where did I shine this week? What did I learn the most about myself, about my confidence this week?

When did I feel most vulnerable this week, and what did I do to feel more safe? Is this a strategy I can use again?

Why did I get in my way, shadow my light?

Who helped me break through a block, to stand strong, or see things in a new way? How?

What one thing will I do differently next week to boost my confidence and add steps toward my goals and dreams?

What am I grateful for this week?

Date:

You can have courage or comfort. You cannot have both.
Brené Brown

Date:

Date:

What am I proud of myself for today?

Date:

Date:

What am I proud of myself for today?

Date:

Date:

What am I proud of myself for today?

Date:

Date:

What am I proud of myself for today?

Date:

Date:

What am I proud of myself for today?

Date:

Date:

What am I proud of myself for today?

Date:

WEEK #7
LOOK BACK

Where did I shine this week? What did I learn the most about myself, about my confidence this week?

When did I feel most vulnerable this week, and what did I do to feel more safe? Is this a strategy I can use again?

WEEK #7
LOOK BACK

Why did I get in my way, shadow my light?

Who helped me break through a block, to stand strong, or see things in a new way? How?

What one thing will I do differently next week to boost my confidence and add steps toward my goals and dreams?

What am I grateful for this week?

Date:

If you light a lamp for somebody, it will also
brighten your path. *Buddhist saying*

Date:

What am I most grateful for today?

Date:

What am I proud of myself for today?

Date:

Date:

What am I proud of myself for today?

Date:

Date:

What am I proud of myself for today?

Date:

Date:

What am I proud of myself for today?

Date:

Date:

What am I proud of myself for today?

Date:

Date:

What am I proud of myself for today?

Date:

WEEK #8
LOOK BACK

Where did I shine this week? What did I learn the most about myself, about my confidence this week?

When did I feel most vulnerable this week, and what did I do to feel more safe? Is this a strategy I can use again?

WEEK #8
LOOK BACK

Why did I get in my way, shadow my light?

Who helped me break through a block, to stand strong, or see things in a new way? How?

What one thing will I do differently next week to boost my confidence and add steps toward my goals and dreams?

What am I grateful for this week?

Date:

Spend time every day in good company.
Your own. *Anonymous*

Date:

Date:

What am I proud of myself for today?

Date:

Date:

What am I proud of myself for today?

Date:

Date:

What am I proud of myself for today?

Date:

Date:

What am I proud of myself for today?

Date:

WEEK # 8 1/2
LOOK BACK

Where did I shine this week? What did I learn the most about myself, about my confidence this week?

When did I feel most vulnerable this week, and what did I do to feel more safe? Is this a strategy I can use again?

Why did I get in my way, shadow my light?

Who helped me break through a block, to stand strong, or see things in a new way? How?

What one thing will I do differently next week to boost my confidence and add steps toward my goals and dreams?

What am I grateful for this week?

My *60-Day* Discovery Summary
Who am I Being in My Life and Business Now?

You've come to the end of your 60-day journey. Congratulations! It's time to reflect on how you've grown, where you're allowing yourself to shine more, and what you want to focus on next. Be as specific as you can.

What, if anything, has shifted in the past 60 days in each of the roles I wrote down in the beginning?

ROLE	True Self Shines	More work to do

MY *60-DAY* DISCOVERY SUMMARY

WHO AM I BEING IN MY LIFE AND BUSINESS NOW?

My *60-Day* Discovery Summary

Who am I Being in My Life and Business Now?

MY *60-DAY* DISCOVERY SUMMARY

MY PLAN FOR MOVING FORWARD

MY *60-DAY* DISCOVERY SUMMARY
WHO IS ON MY "LIGHT SHINE" SUPPORT TEAM?

My *60-Day* Discovery Summary

My Favorite Quotes or Affirmations That Keep My Light Shining Bright

Affirmation

I am no longer afraid to play BIG! I no longer choose to dim my light and hide in the shadows. I refuse to leave this earth with my gifts inside me. From here forward I will be loud and proud about who I am and the value I bring. The world needs me to shine my radiant light!

ABOUT THE AUTHOR

Erin Summ, CPC, supports shy and introverted women entrepreneurs to step past their fears of being seen and heard, to release their limiting beliefs, to stand in confidence and shine their brilliant light, leaving their impact on the world.

Formerly a shy woman, having battled many of her own limiting beliefs and gremlins, Erin is now a sought after confidence coach, workshop leader, and speaker.

"My intentions for you ~ to replace the fear of being seen and heard with the confidence to shine your own brilliant, unique light. To bask in unconditional self-love and respect and to share this with your loved ones, community and the world."

FIND OUT MORE ABOUT ERIN'S ONE-ON-ONE
COACHING, COURSES, BOOKS,
PUBLIC SPEAKING, AND FREE VIDEO TIPS
www.erinsumm.com

Made in the USA
San Bernardino, CA
10 November 2016